I0817394

EARTH'S PRECIOUS

WATER

AN ALTERNATIVE ENERGY SOURCE

by John Perritano

Go to **www.openlightbox.com**, and enter this book's unique code.

ACCESS CODE

LBXU5259

Lightbox is an all-inclusive digital solution for the teaching and learning of curriculum topics in an original, groundbreaking way. Lightbox is based on National Curriculum Standards.

STANDARD FEATURES OF LIGHTBOX

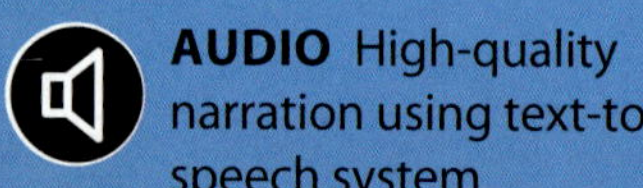
AUDIO High-quality narration using text-to-speech system

ACTIVITIES Printable PDFs that can be emailed and graded

SLIDESHOWS Pictorial overviews of key concepts

VIDEOS Embedded high-definition video clips

WEBLINKS Curated links to external, child-safe resources

TRANSPARENCIES Step-by-step layering of maps, diagrams, charts, and timelines

INTERACTIVE MAPS Interactive maps and aerial satellite imagery

QUIZZES Ten multiple choice questions that are automatically graded and emailed for teacher assessment

KEY WORDS Matching key concepts to their definitions

Contents

Water as a Source of Energy

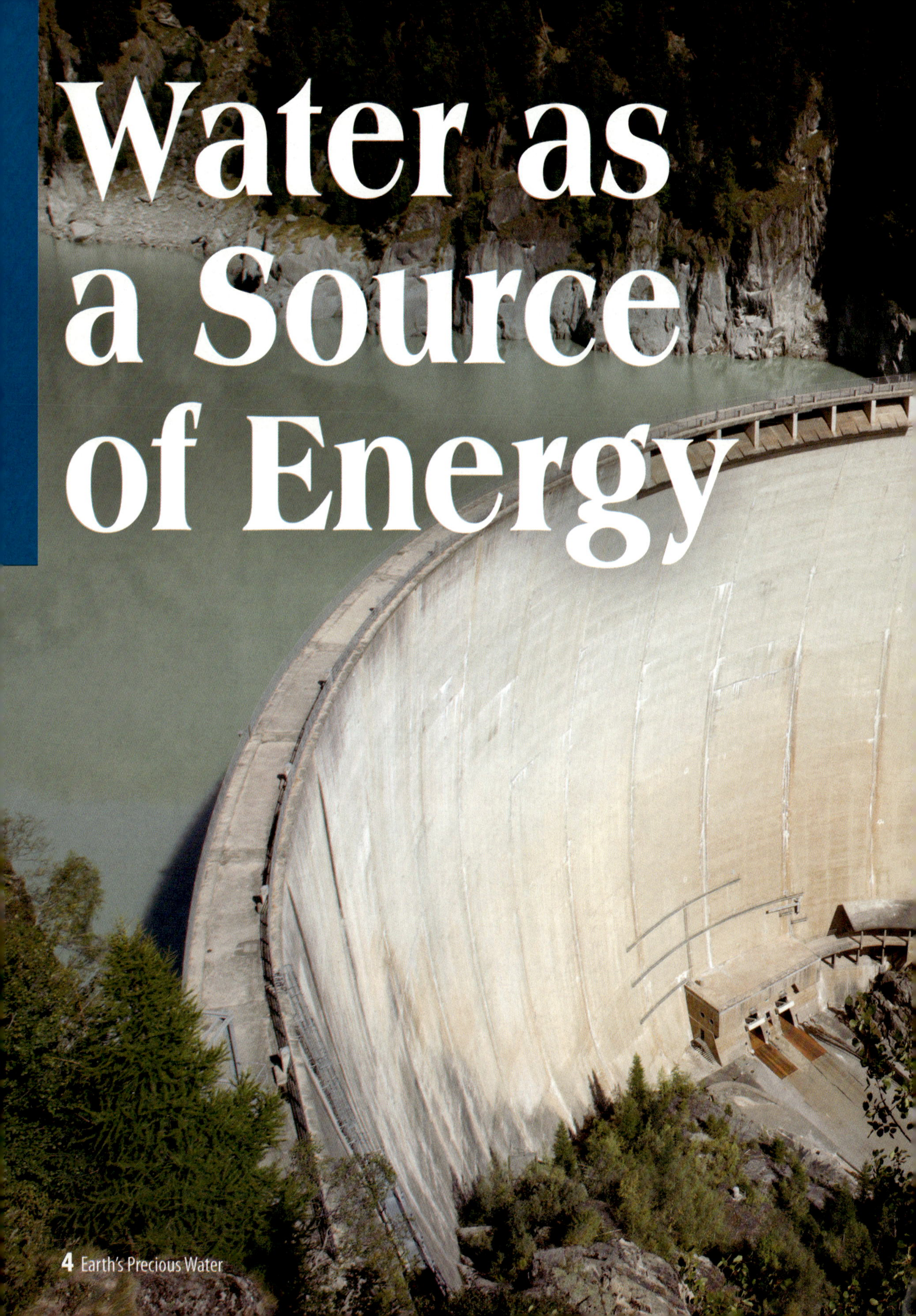

Most people use electricity every day. They need it to watch television, text their friends, light their room, and keep cool in the summer and warm in the winter. Many people do not realize how much they need electricity until they do not have it any longer.

Today, power plants create most of the electricity people need. However, not all power plants are the same. Some use **fossil fuels** to create an electrical charge. Oil, coal, and natural gas are fossil fuels. They are nonrenewable resources. Once they run out, they are gone. Nearly 91 percent of all the energy Americans use comes from nonrenewable fuels.

Some power stations use renewable sources of energy. Renewable sources are those that will not run out. The Sun, for example, is a source of renewable energy. **Solar cells** turn the Sun's rays into electricity.

Moving water can be used to generate hydroelectric power. This power is another important source of renewable energy. Today, nearly 25 percent of the world's electricity comes from hydroelectric power. Hydroelectric power is the largest source of renewable energy on Earth. Each year, rainfall and snow melt fills rivers and streams. This water rushes through hydroelectric power plants. Those plants use machines called **turbines** to generate electricity. Unlike oil and coal, hydropower is clean to make and use.

Norway gets **99 percent** of its electricity from **waterpower**.

The **largest** U.S. hydroelectric plant is the **6,800-megawatt Grand Coulee power station**, in Washington state.

About **9.4 percent of energy** used in the United States comes from **renewable** sources.

Early Forms of Water Power

The women of ancient Greece used their hands to pound wheat into flour. It was a hard, back-breaking job. Then, one day, someone figured out that a wheel could capture the power of running water. This technology, the waterwheel, changed the course of human history.

Early waterwheels had a set of wooden panels that trapped rushing water. The water pounded against the panels, turning the wheel. People hooked up the waterwheel to a millstone. This large, circular stone mashed grain into flour as it turned. Waterwheels were also used to power saws that cut through wood. Other waterwheels were used to help turn wool into fabric for clothes.

The Greeks were not the only people to use the waterwheel. The ancient Romans used them, as did the Chinese. The use of waterwheels spread throughout Europe. One record, published in 1016, listed 6,000 waterwheel-powered mills in England alone. Using the energy contained in rushing water as a source of power made work easier. As the centuries passed, scientists and inventors found better ways to use water as a source of power.

The Chinese used waterwheels to collect water for their crops.

In 1837, Benoit Fourneyron developed a turbine with 10 times more power than his first design.

In the United States, Fourneyron turbines were installed on Niagara falls to generate electricity in 1895.

Francis turbines can be used either upright or on their sides.

The Electric Turbine

When: 1800–1849 | **Where:** Europe and North America

For centuries, people knew that electricity existed, but they did not know very much about it. In 1800, an inventor named Alessandro Volta proved that electricity could travel over wires. About 27 years later, a French engineer named Benoit Fourneyron built an electric turbine powered by rushing water which caused blades connected to a shaft to spin. His turbine produced as much power as six horses. In 1849, an engineer named James Francis invented the first modern turbine. People still use it today.

DISCUSSION

Why would the Francis turbine still be used today? Think about what this can tell you about waterwheel technology.

Water enters a Francis turbine through the side and exits through the middle.

The biggest Francis turbines can weigh more than 450 tons (408 metric tons).

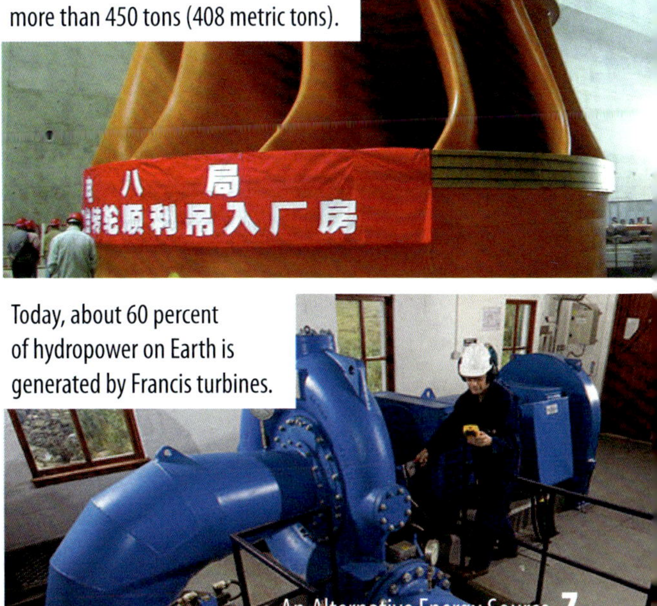

Today, about 60 percent of hydropower on Earth is generated by Francis turbines.

When it was completed in 1935, the Hoover Dam changed the course of the Colorado River. It created a huge body of water—Lake Mead.

Hydroelectric Dams

Southeast of Las Vegas, Nevada, is a modern marvel. It sits in a place called the Black Canyon. Its name is the Hoover Dam. A dam is a structure built across a body of water to hold back water. As a hydroelectric dam, the Hoover dam is also able to use this water to generate electricity. This U-shaped dam provides millions of people with electricity.

Standing at 726 feet (221.28 m) tall and 1,244 feet (379.17 m) long, the Hoover Dam was once one of the largest human-made structures in the world. It was also one of the planet's largest producers of hydroelectric power.

Many hydroelectric dams, including Hoover Dam, are gravity fed. That means water rushes downward into these dams from **reservoirs** through a series of large pipes called penstocks. This rushing water slams into the blades of electric turbines located at the bottom of gravity fed dams.

The force of the water causes a turbine's blades to spin. The spinning turbine in turn spins a shaft in a device known as a generator. The generator uses the spinning shaft to create electricity. This electricity is transferred to where it can be used or stored using transmission lines.

Transmission lines can be used to send power across borders. This occurs at the Itaipu Dam, which sends power to Paraguay and Brazil. The dam produces 103 billion kilowatt-hours of hydroelectricity each year, more than any other hydroelectric dam on Earth.

Some hydroelectric plants use pumped storage. During times when little electricity is needed, power is used to pump water back into the reservoir. Once more power is needed again, the water is allowed to flow back through the turbines.

Dams on rivers produce most of the world's hydroelectricity. Each year, Hoover Dam generates about 4 billion kilowatt-hours of hydroelectricity. That is enough electricity to serve 1.3 billion people.

At its base, Hoover Dam **is as thick** as **two football fields**.

Hoover Dam is almost **200 feet** (61 m) **taller** than the Washington Monument.

Hoover Dam has **17 main** electric turbines.

Tidal Power

As a wave moves toward shore, shallow water causes the wave to break forward.

When people go swimming in the ocean, they should be aware that an incoming wave can knock them down. Moreover, the outgoing tide can drag people from shore. The ocean is very powerful. Tidal power plants harness the **kinetic energy** of the tides and turn it into electricity.

Tides are generated by the **gravitational** pull of the Sun and Moon, along with the rotation of Earth. The most noticeable tides are caused by the Moon. There are both high tides and low tides. As the tides move in and out, they create currents along coastal areas. Those currents contain a large amount of kinetic energy. More than 10 centuries ago, people living in coastal Europe used the tides to drive grain mills. Today, tidal power stations harness the energy contained in these currents to drive electrical turbines.

The La Rance Tidal Power Station

The La Rance Tidal Power Station, in France, was the first tidal power plant in the world. Workers built the plant where the Rance River meets the English Channel.

Date of Completion: 1966
Total Turbines: 24

Installed Capacity: 240 MW
Yearly Production: 500 gigawatt hours

Tidal barrage power plants are similar to dams. The dam, known as a barrage, holds the ocean water back. When the tide is high, workers open special "sluice" gates, allowing the tide to rush in. This water spins turbines and makes electricity.

Another way to generate electricity from the ocean is to install tidal turbines on the seafloor in places where the tide is strong. These turbines look like undersea wind turbines. The turbines generate electricity when the flowing current of the tide strikes their underwater blades as it moves in and out.

The first tidal power project in the United States began delivering power to the state of Maine in 2012. The turbine looks like the blades of an old-fashioned lawn mower. They rotate when the tide rushes in and out of Cobscook Bay, near Eastport. The plant can power 25 to 30 homes.

TIDAL TURBINES

Tidal turbines work just like those in river dams. Moving water strikes the turbine, spinning its blades. The turbine is connected to a generator, which produces electricity. All that power is then transmitted over wires to cities and towns.

1. Gravitational Pull

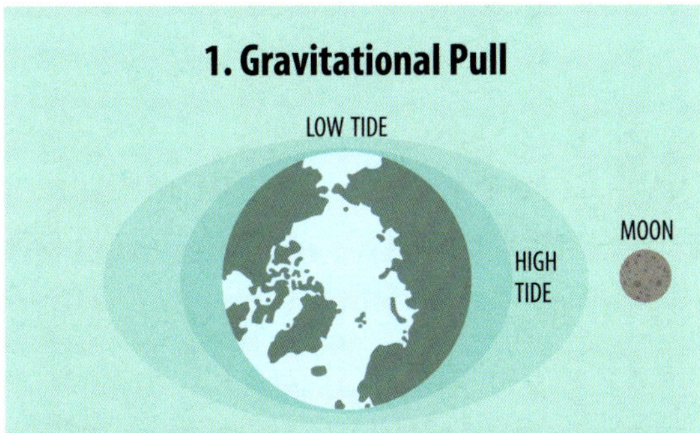

The Moon's gravity pulls on the oceans as it orbits Earth. The ocean bulges out on the side closest to the moon and the side farthest from the Moon. When that happens, high tides are created.

2. Incoming Tide

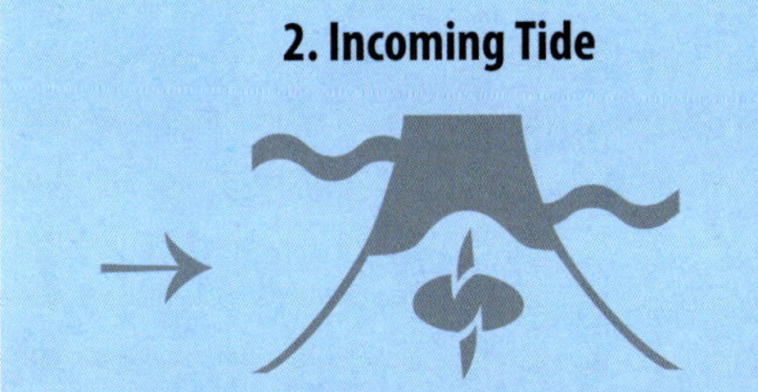

Tidal turbines work best when they are built between two slabs of land in a narrow channel. When the high tide funnels in, water rises on one side of the channel and pours out the other side. As that happens, the turbines spin, generating electricity.

3. Outgoing Tide

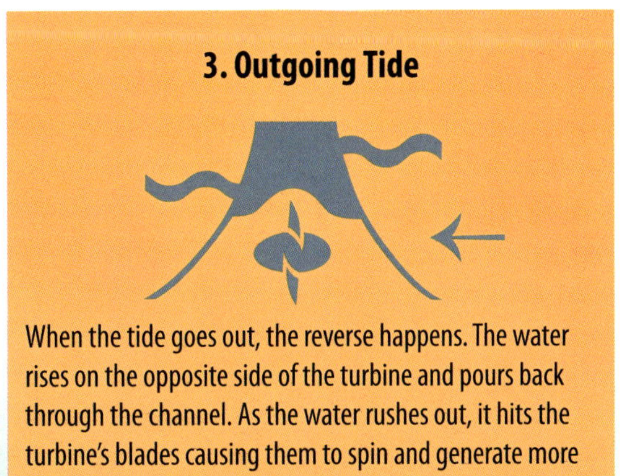

When the tide goes out, the reverse happens. The water rises on the opposite side of the turbine and pours back through the channel. As the water rushes out, it hits the turbine's blades causing them to spin and generate more electricity.

The Future of Water Power

New York City's East River runs between Manhattan and Brooklyn. It is a strange place to produce electricity. However, In September of 2012, a company sank a special three-bladed electric turbine into the waterway. The device looked like a torpedo with a fan. The turbine used the push and pull of the river's rushing current to spin the fan and make electricity. One day, these turbines may be able to power hundreds of homes.

The use of tidal turbines in the ocean is increasing, with many of them being placed into the ocean with the help of large cranes. Cables along the seabed take power that is generated from these turbines to the shore.

Turbines are only one of several hydropower **innovations** that may bring this ancient power source into the future. Harnessing the rushing power of river water tops the list. In California, a company has invented a system that uses the kinetic energy all along a river rather than in just one spot, as dams do.

Workers string several modules across a river. Each of these modules is an electric turbine with a propeller. Very strong steel cables hold the modules in place. Flowing water passes through the turbines, driving a generator. This system can generate 50 kilowatts in river water that is moving at 4.6 miles (7.4 km) per hour. The system is also low impact. It does not affect how birds and fish use rivers to move around.

Harnessing Energy from a Slow River

In 2007, a professor at the University of Michigan studied how fish swim and figured out how to harness a slowly-moving river's kinetic energy. He invented a device he calls **Vortex** Induced Vibration for Aquatic Clean Energy (VIVACE). When fish move through water, they curve their bodies. As they do, they create tiny swirling whirlpools. Fish push against these tiny whirlpools to move themselves forward. VIVACE works the same way.

1 Whirlpools of Energy

The river's slow current flows over boxes of cylinders on the river bottom. As the current passes over the cylinders, tiny whirlpools called vortices form. The water's circular movement makes the cylinders go up and down.

2 Direct Current

Inside each cylinder is a magnet. That magnet moves over a metal coil. As the magnet moves, it produces a type of electrical charge called direct current (DC). A battery powering a flashlight is an example of direct current at work.

3 Usable Energy

VIVACE then takes the DC current and changes it into alternating current (AC). That makes it easier and safer to transmit over powerlines to homes and businesses. Engineers have been experimenting with VIVACE on rivers in Michigan.

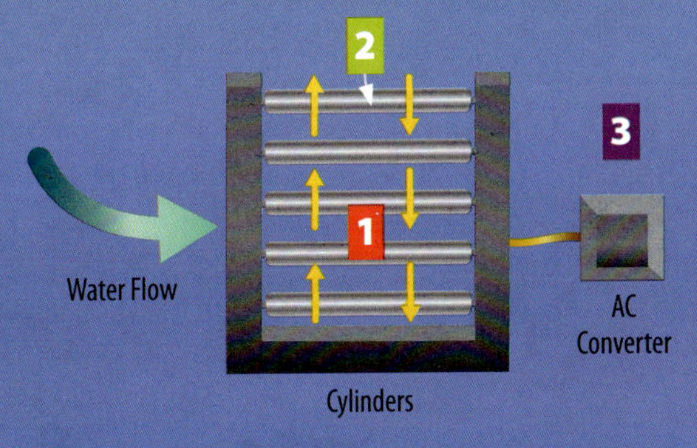

Environmental Problems

There are nearly 40,000 large dams around the world. They have helped people improve their lives. Dams have irrigated fields, helped the poor, and have prevented famines from occurring in otherwise dry areas. They are a well-known source of clean power.

However, hydroelectric dams can also cause problems. In many cases, they have destroyed **ecosystems** by changing the flow of water and creating new lakes. They can block migration routes used by fish. When dams are built, they can uproot millions from their homes.

Many hydroelectric dams build fish ladders that allow salmon to jump upstream.

The Three Gorges Dam, in China, is the world's largest hydroelectric dam. However, it is also considered by some to be one of the most destructive dams on the planet. It was built on the Yangtze River to generate electricity and help develop industry. However, the dam's reservoir destroyed villages and flooded forests and farms. The loss of all this land led to **erosion** problems that destroyed the habitats of many animals, including the Siberian crane, the Chinese tiger, and the giant panda. The dam also caused toxic water, from factories that dumped waste into the river, to flood over a large area.

About 1,300 historic sites were flooded by the Three Gorges Dam reservoir.

Large dams can also have a positive effect. Supporters of these dams argue that they save the environment by creating less pollution than fossil-fuel plants. Dams also produce hydroelectricity efficiently. While a typical fossil fuel plant converts about 50 percent of available energy into electricity, a large-scale hydropower plant converts about 90 percent. Many countries want to build large dams. On the Yangtze alone, some 15 dams are planned, under construction, or completed.

Today, about 66 percent of the planet's possible hydropower remains unused. That is why companies and governments want to build more hydroelectric dams. Experts estimate that hydropower will grow by about 3 percent per year during the next few decades.

The Three Gorges Dam is **1.4 miles** (2.3 km) long and **607 feet** (185 m) wide.

The Three Gorges Dam's **reservoir** is **574 feet** (175 m) above sea level.

More than **1.3 million people had to leave their homes** due to the construction of the Three Gorges Dam.

Hydroelectric Engineers

A hydroelectric engineer has many jobs. They design, build, and operate hydropower facilities. Engineers, along with technicians, make sure the water and electricity are always flowing properly. Engineers are responsible for maintaining and repairing equipment. They must solve complex problems. They need to know why a piece of equipment fails and how to fix it.

Hydroelectricity History

4,000 years ago

The ancient Greeks develop a waterwheel to grind grain.

1849

James Francis builds the first modern water turbine. It includes shaped blades to make sure water enters the turbine at the right angle. The design is so successful that hydroelectric power plants still use it today.

1878

The first hydroelectric project lights a lamp in a house in Northumberland, Great Britain. Four years later, the first hydroelectric plant to serve American customers opens in Wisconsin.

Hydroelectric engineers need many skills. They work with hand tools and power tools. They must know how to read blueprints and other technical drawings. Engineers must also effectively communicate with others. Hydroelectric plants have pipes, tunnels, circuits, and switches. That is why an engineer working at the plant must also know a lot about both plumbing and electricity. A hydroelectric engineer must also make sure the power plant follows all government regulations and rules.

The person who is responsible for running the hydroelectric plant is called a plant manager. It is the plant manager's responsibility to make sure the plant is running smoothly and that the electricity is always turned on.

1882

The first power plant at Niagara Falls, N.Y., begins operation, but in two years it fails. Other power plants soon begin generating electricity near the falls.

1930

Construction of the Hoover Dam begins. After six years, the dam, known at the time as Boulder Dam, opens.

2017

About 6.3 percent of electricity in the United States comes from hydropower. The country is the third-largest producer of hydropower on Earth.

Notable Hydroelectric Locations

1 Washington State, United States

Washington state is the largest producer and consumer of hydroelectric power in the United States. Nearly 66 percent of the state's electric companies receive their power from hydroelectric plants. The largest power plants are on the Columbia and Snake rivers.

2 Tennessee River Valley, United States

In the 1930s, U.S. President Franklin Roosevelt wanted to bring electricity to the Tennessee River Valley. The valley included portions of several states. Roosevelt believed a series of dams along Tennessee River would bring jobs to the region. Today, the Tennessee River Valley Authority is the largest public power company in the United States.

3 Itaipu Dam, Brazil and Paraguay

Located on the border between Brazil and Paraguay, the Itaipu hydroelectric dam is one of the largest on Earth. However, its construction has been controversial. Thousands of people in the area were forced to leave their homes when the dam was built.

4 MeyGen Tidal Stream Project, Great Britain

In 2016, workers began building the world's first large-scale underwater tidal energy farm. Located off the coast of Scotland in a strait called the Pentland Firth, this plant may generate enough electricity to replace three coal power plants. The builders of the plant hope to install 269 turbines, which can generate enough electricity to power 175,000 homes.

5 Aswan Dam, Egypt

Before workers began building the Aswan Dam in Egypt in 1960, they had to do some heavy lifting. Construction of the dam threatened a series of ancient temples, which had been built centuries earlier into the sides of cliffs. The government relocated an entire mountainside to a nearby hill to preserve these ancient relics.

6 Sihwa Lake, South Korea

The world's largest tidal power plant is located on Sihwa Lake in South Korea. The plant opened in 2011, near the city of Siheung. The plant consists of a 7-mile (12.5-km) seawall. When the tide flows in, it spins 10 turbines which generate 552.7 gigawatt hours of electricity each year.

Proposing a Hydroelectric Dam

People and governments make decisions on where to build hydroelectric plants. Research online and in the library how people in your community or state have dealt with a proposal to build a hydroelectric dam, or some other hydroelectric facility.

WHAT HAPPENED?

Whose idea was the project? What type of hydroelectric facility was proposed? Research its size and what people hoped would happen once the project was built.

WHAT WAS THE EFFECT?

Who supported the project? Why? Who opposed the project? Why? Were there any environmental concerns? If so, what were they? What did people say about the plan?

WHAT ACTIONS WERE TAKEN?

Research the decisions that were made and describe the outcome. Did the project get built? What were the effects? What changes were made to the project after everyone gave their opinion?

Gravity, Water, and Energy

Instructions

Step 1: Fill a cup of water. Place the newspaper on the floor.

Step 2: Have a partner hold a meter stick upright near the cup.

Step 3: Put the straw into the cup of water. Place a finger over the top of the straw so the water does not fall out.

Step 4: Hold the straw near the meter stick. Record on a piece of paper how high the straw is being held. Release your finger from the top of the straw.

Step 5: Record the length of the splash. Repeat at different levels of heights. Make sure the amount of water in the straw is the same for each round.

Step 6: Study the data you recorded. What is the relationship between distance and the length of the splash? At what height does the water have the greatest potential energy?

Materials

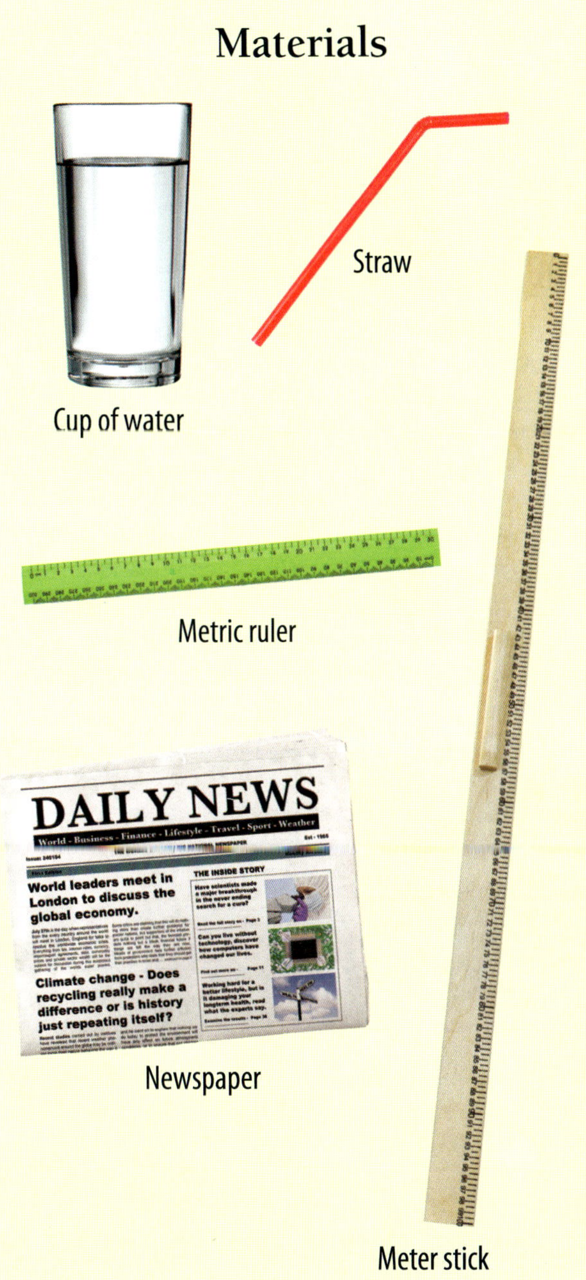

Quiz

Test your knowledge by answering these questions. All of the information can be found in the text you just read. The answers are provided below for easy reference.

1. What was the first device that was able to harness the power of rushing water?
2. What amount of the world's electricity comes from hydroelectric power stations?
3. What is a nonrenewable resource?
4. Is water a renewable resource?
5. Who invented the modern turbine?
6. Where is Sihwa Lake located?
7. Where is the world's largest hydroelectric dam?
8. What do tidal power plants harness to create electricity?
9. What does a generator do?
10. Which U.S. state produces the most hydroelectric power?

ANSWER KEY

1. The waterwheel **2.** 25 percent **3.** A resource that will eventually run out **4.** Yes **5.** James Francis **6.** South Korea **7.** China **8.** Energy from the tides **9.** Creates electricity **10.** Washington

Key Words

ecosystems: communities where different organisms live

erosion: the wearing-away of a surface

fossil fuels: nonrenewable energy sources, such as coal, oil, and natural gas, formed by the fossilized remains of plants and animals that lived millions of years ago

gravitational: the force of attraction between two objects, such as Earth and the Moon

innovations: actions or processes that involve altering or rearranging something to create something new and better

kinetic energy: energy an object possesses due to its motion

reservoirs: a natural or artificial lake used as a water supply

solar cells: a device that produces electricity from the Sun's rays

turbines: machines, with wheels and rotors, that produce a continuous source of electricity

vortex: a mass of whirling fluid

Index

LIGHTBOX

SUPPLEMENTARY RESOURCES

Click on the plus icon ⊕ found in the bottom left corner of each spread to open additional teacher resources.

- Download and print the book's quizzes and activities
- Access curriculum correlations
- Explore additional web applications that enhance the Lightbox experience

LIGHTBOX DIGITAL TITLES
Packed full of integrated media

VIDEOS

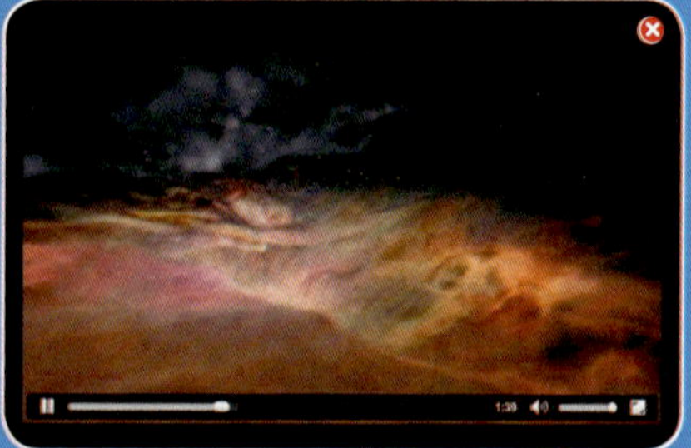

INTERACTIVE MAPS

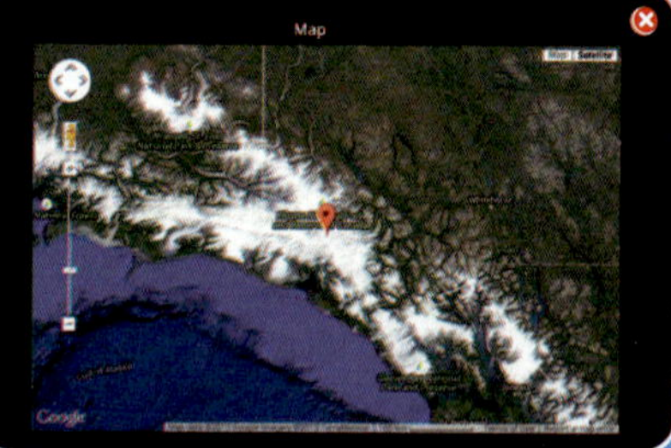

WEBLINKS

SLIDESHOWS

QUIZZES

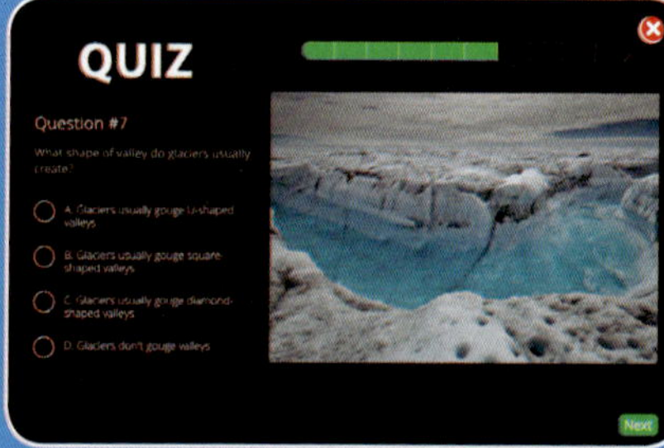

OPTIMIZED FOR
- ✓ TABLETS
- ✓ WHITEBOARDS
- ✓ COMPUTERS
- ✓ AND MUCH MORE!

Published by Smartbook Media Inc.
350 5th Avenue, 59th Floor
New York, NY 10118
Website: www.openlightbox.com

Library of Congress Control Number:
2018944574

ISBN 978-1-5105-3887-0 (hardcover)
ISBN 978-1-5105-3888-7 (multi-user eBook)

Printed in Brainerd, Minnesota, United States
1 2 3 4 5 6 7 8 9 0 22 21 20 19 18

072018
120517

Project Coordinator John Willis
Art Director Terry Paulhus

Photo Credits
Every reasonable effort has been made to trace ownership and to obtain permission to reprint copyright material. The publisher would be pleased to have any errors or omissions brought to its attention so that they may be corrected in subsequent printings. The publisher acknowledges Alamy, Getty Images, iStock, Shutterstock, and Wikimedia as its primary image suppliers for this title.